Department of the Environment
Ancient Monuments and Historic

Orford Castle

SUFFOLK

R. ALLEN BROWN MA, D Phil, FSA

LONDON: HER MAJESTY'S STATIONERY OFFICE

Contents

First published 1964

Eighth impression 1978

ISBN 0 11 670070 X

Map to show castles mentioned in the text

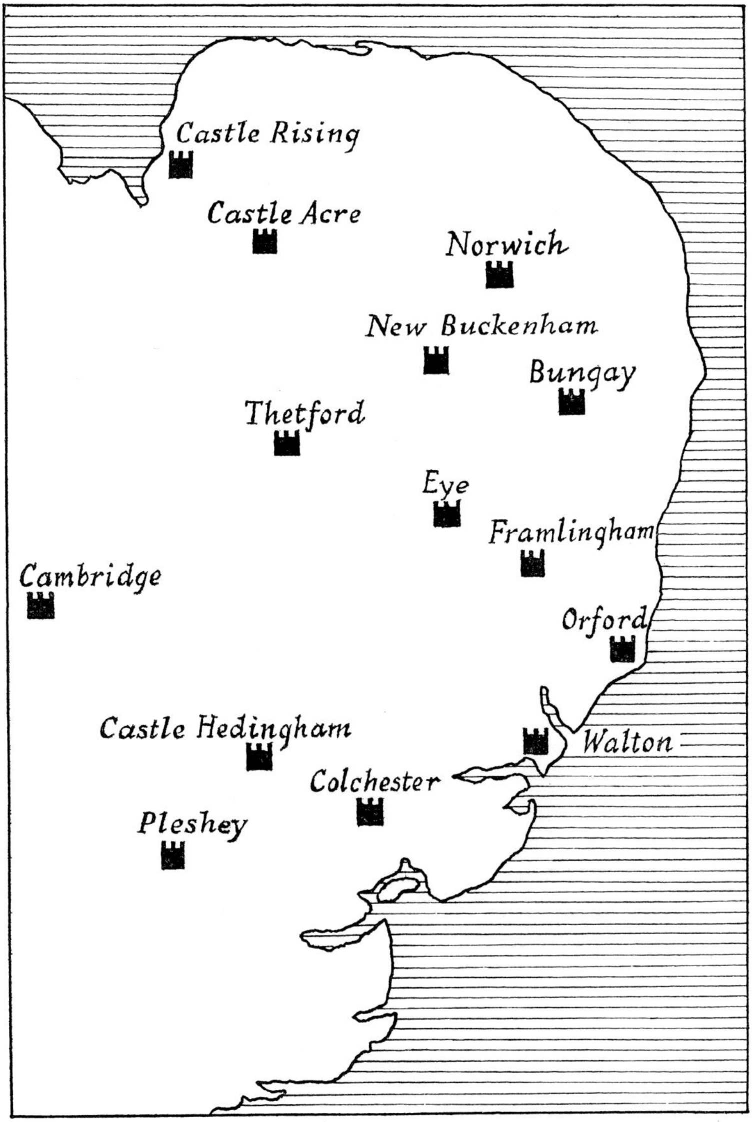

History

Orford Castle, on the Suffolk coast, has two special claims to interest: first, the unique design of its great tower or keep (now all that survives above ground of the castle), and, second, the fact that it is the earliest castle in the kingdom for whose building documentary evidence survives. This evidence is found upon the Pipe Rolls, the great annual rolls of the medieval exchequer, the financial department of the King's government, which year by year contain the accounts of the sheriffs, who were the royal officials in charge of the shires or counties, and of certain other royal bailiffs in charge of lesser districts. The first extant Pipe Roll dates from 1130 in the reign of Henry I, and thereafter they survive in almost unbroken series from the reign of Henry II (1154–89) onwards. Since Orford Castle was founded and built by Henry II, therefore, we are able to say with precision that the work began in the accounting year Michaelmas 1165 to Michaelmas 1166, and was completed by the year 1172-73, at a total recorded cost of £1413 9s 2d. Though at first sight this figure may seem more comic than impressive, it was, of course, a very great sum of money in a period when the total basic revenues of the Crown have been estimated at less than £10 000 a year, when the constable of the new castle at Orford might receive £20 a year as the wages for his responsible and dignified office, or when 1d a day was the normal wage for the porters and watchmen of the King's castles. In fact, the total cost of Orford exceeds that of almost all the other extensive castle works carried out by Henry II, and though the prodigious cost of the rebuilding of Dover Castle in this period soars far above it (some £7000 between 1168 and 1191), Dover was exceptional. King John, by contrast, was able to build his new castle at Odiham in Hampshire between 1207 and 1214 at a total recorded cost of some £1200.

Unfortunately, the Pipe Rolls give few details of the nature of the building, the usual type of entry being simply, 'In the work of the castle of Orford, so many pounds, by the authority of the King's writ, and by the view of so and so.' The function of the 'viewers' at this date was to check the sheriff's expenditure, and to certify at the exchequer that he had in fact spent the amount he claimed and in the manner in which he asserted. Those who acted as viewers of the works at Orford were usually Bartholomew de Glanville and Robert de Valoines (both local landowners of substance and related to the better-known Ranulf de Glanville, founder of Leiston Abbey and Butley Priory and later to be the King's Chief Justiciar), together with Wimar the chaplain (who was to be perpetual vicar of the church at Orford now also building). The Pipe Rolls do, however, make it very clear that the work was pressed on with considerable speed. In the first year, 1165–66, a total of over £663 was spent—by far the largest sum spent upon any one building in any one year so far recorded for Henry II's reign—and by the end of the first two years, 1165–67, the total expenditure was close on £1000 (£986 9s 8d). It is evident also that by this time some substantial part of the castle had already been completed, for in 1167 a payment of 38s 4d was made for the 'munition of the castle' —i.e. the provision of supplies for it—and 20 marks (£13 6s 8d) were paid to Bartholomew de Glanville as its first constable. That the first part of the castle to be finished was in fact the present keep may be suggested with some confidence. One would expect the keep to be built before the curtain walls which were eventually to surround it (this, for example, was the sequence followed at Dover in the 1180s and in 1204 King John wrote to the Justiciar of Ireland about the new castle at Dublin, and ordered him to build the keep first and the rest of the castle afterwards); while the sum of £986 so far spent at Orford accords very well with the recorded cost of some £912 for another of Henry II's great keeps, that of Newcastle upon Tyne, built between *c*1172 and 1177. If the keep at Orford was indeed completed in the two years 1165–67, then this was a very impressive achievement, and one which would seem to point to the importance attached by the King to the building of his new castle. Thereafter work continued until 1173, presumably upon the walls, towers and other defences of the bailey and such buildings within it as were necessary in addition to the keep. £120 was spent in 1167–68 and £134 in 1168–69, in which latter year timber was brought from as far away as Scarborough in Yorkshire where another keep was being built in the royal castle there. In the next few years the level of expenditure at Orford slowly declined, until on the Pipe Roll of 1172–73, we find the last entry relating to the construction of the new castle, 'And in the work of one great ditch about the castle of Orford with palisades and bratices and in the work of the stone bridge of the said castle £58 2s 8d by the writ of Richard de Luci the Justiciar and by the view of Robert de Valoines and two Normans of Ipswich.'

In the year 1173 in which Orford was completed, a serious rebellion against Henry II, led by his eldest son, the 'Young King,' broke out both in England and in the King's continental dominions. Orford

Castle, in fact, was built just in time to uphold the King's authority in Suffolk, which was one of the principal theatres of the rebellion. These facts must surely be relevant to any consideration of why Henry II chose to raise a new castle at this point on the Suffolk coast and at this time. Although Orford was evidently already in the mid-twelfth century a flourishing port (at this date the great spit of Orford Ness ended at a point roughly opposite the town, to shelter the haven and not block it by its long southerly extension as now) there is little doubt that the King's motives were chiefly political. We must therfore examine the political situation in Suffolk and East Anglia in the early years of Henry's reign.

The warfare of this period largely turned upon castles because castles literally dominated the land. If you wished to control the land, you had first to control the castles. A contemporary chronicler, William of Newburgh, called the royal castles of England 'the bones of the kingdom'; but at any time in the twelfth century royal castles were heavily outnumbered by baronial. Hence the political importance of castles in an age when political opposition to the King could, and did, appeal to arms. When Henry II became King in 1154, there were, in fact, no royal castles in East Anglia, though the district was thickly planted with the castles of the great magnates who had lands and honours here. Among the greatest of these great men was Hugh Bigod, created earl of Norfolk by King Stephen. In 1154 Earl Hugh held four East Anglian castles—Bungay and Framlingham, Walton (now vanished) and Thetford—and further, since his earldom of Norfolk was in reality the older earldom of the East Angles, he had claims upon Norwich, the ancient capital of that earldom as it is still the capital of East Anglia. At first, upon Henry II's accession, all was well, and Hugh Bigod was reappointed to his earldom in 1155. But in 1157 Henry, no doubt feeling secure upon the throne, confiscated from William, King Stephen's son (whose instatement in these and other lordships had been one of the conditions whereby Henry's claims to the kingdom had been recognised), the East Anglian fortresses of Eye, Castle Acre and Norwich itself, and in the same year took all four of his castles from Earl Hugh. Exactly how and why the latter confiscation was carried out is unknown, but that it was done there is no doubt. So matters remained until 1165 when, evidently in return for an extremely heavy fine of £1000 made with the King at Nottingham, Earl Hugh received back his two castles of Framlingham and Bungay, but not

Aerial view of the keep from the east

The castle from the south-west, from John Norden's Survey of the Manor of Sudbourne, 1600–02

Walton and Thetford which were retained in royal hands. It was in 1165 also, as we have seen, that the new royal castle at Orford was begun, to be finished just before the outbreak of the rebellion of 1173–74. It is not surprising to find that Earl Hugh Bigod, though then some eighty years of age, was amongst the leaders of that revolt (as the price of his support he was promised the castles of Norwich and Eye), and rather sad to relate that the outcome was his defeat, and the demolition of his remaining castles of Bungay and Framlingham, with Thetford and Walton. There can, moreover, be no doubt that these stirring circumstances point to the political motives behind the building of Orford Castle, while the military and therefore political value of the castle in the context of twelfth-century East Anglia is further emphasised when it is noted that Orford stands between Framlingham and the sea, and that the Suffolk coast then as ever was the invasion coast, by which, in fact, the Flemish mercenaries brought over by Bigod and his allies in 1173 to fight King Henry entered the kingdom.

The King's new castle of Orford, then, played an important part in upholding royal authority in Suffolk in the rebellion of 1173–74. It was garrisoned and provisioned for the Crown, over £159 being paid out in wages to the knights and sergeants within it in the former year. Supplies of all kinds were brought in, bacons, cheeses and salt, iron, ropes and tallow, hand-mills to grind corn, and also coal—some of which was captured by the Flemings on its way to the castle. In 1174 the Pipe Roll refers not only to continuing payments to the garrison of Orford, but also to compensation paid to a certain Ralph the Breton 'for his houses which were carried into the castle,' no doubt to provide the extra accommodation needed in such an emergency. There is no record of the castle thus fortified being attacked by the rebels, though minor repairs were carried out upon it when the fighting was over.

After this dramatic start to its military history, Orford continued to be an important royal castle for almost 200 years, held for the King by a royal constable who was often, but not always, the sheriff; a centre of local government, a symbol of royal authority in an important East Anglian port, and garrisoned and provisioned when trouble threatened or occurred. Thus it was garrisoned again in 1192–93 during the political upheavals at the time of Richard I's absence on Crusade, and once more became a base and centre of active military operations in the rebellion which closed the reign of John. Soon after the sealing of Magna Carta in the summer of 1215, King John placed Orford in the custody of no less a person than Hubert de Burgh, the Justiciar, who was to win fame and honour in the ensuing warfare by his defence of Dover Castle against the rebels. In March 1216 the King wrote to Hubert's deputy-constable authorising him to admit into the castle, as and when necessary, the force of Savaric de Mauléon, sent into Suffolk to attack the King's enemies there. Savaric de Mauléon (now Chatillon-sur-Sèvre) was prominent among John's 'alien' captains and was in fact an adventurous knight, baron and troubadour from Poitou, of which he had been the King's seneschal. In the same month John himself was in Suffolk, conducting a lightning campaign against East Anglian rebel castles, in the course of which he took, among others, Framlingham, by this time rebuilt in the form in which it now stands, and held against him by Roger Bigod, Earl of Norfolk, son and heir of the unfortunate Earl Hugh. In the following year, 1217, after the death of King John at Newark Castle in Nottinghamshire, the tide of war in East Anglia flowed the other way, and Orford itself, together with Cambridge and Colchester, Pleshey and Castle Hedingham, was taken by the French Prince Louis, the appointed leader of the rebel magnates and contender for the throne. Little actual damage to the castle seems to have been done, for when peace and royal authority were restored in the name of the boy King Henry III only small sums were spent upon its repair.

During the political troubles and the Barons' Wars of Henry III's reign, the castle was important enough to change hands frequently in accordance with the varying fortunes of the two parties, the baronial opposition entrusting it twice to Roger Bigod, Earl of Norfolk, and the King to his son, the Lord Edward, and to Philip Marmion. The Lord Edward was given the custody of Orford again by his father in 1272, and, as King, visited the castle on 11 April 1277. Twice more in this period, when rebellion threatened, Orford was ordered to be put in a state of defence, by Edward I in 1297 and by Edward II in 1307–08. Up to this time also it was evidently maintained in good condition. Between 1272 and 1275 £75 was spent in repairs; in 1277–78 lead was bought for two of the four turrets surmounting the keep; and between 1317 and 1318 over £55 was spent upon the repair of the well, and of the houses, walls and other defects of the castle. It is noticeable, however, that at the turn of the thirteenth and fourteenth centuries the castle was repeatedly granted out for life—to Robert of Ufford (the elder) in 1280, to Roger Bigod, Earl of Norfolk, in 1302, to Robert of Ufford (the younger) in 1330—such grants presumably indicating its declining importance in the eyes of the Crown. Finally, in 1336, Edward III granted Orford Castle in perpetuity to Robert of Ufford, who was created Earl of Suffolk in the following year; he was to hold it from the Crown for a peppercorn rent, and his heirs after him for £20 a year. Thenceforward until our own time Orford remained in private hands. It was bought and presented to the Orford Town Trust by the generosity of Sir Arthur Churchman in 1930, and passed into the custody of the State under the provisions of the Ancient Monuments Acts in 1962.

Description

In overall plan Orford Castle was typical enough of its age, and belonged to a type which has been called the keep-and-bailey castle, the stone-built equivalent of the motte-and-bailey, particularly characteristic of the Norman Conquest. It thus had two components, the walled enclosure of the bailey, and the keep, great tower, or donjon, which stood both as a self-contained lordly residence and as an independent, ultimate strong-point or citadel, which could be defended even if the rest of the castle, i.e. the bailey, should fall. (This, for example, was the pattern of the defence of Rochester Castle in the siege of 1215, and of Bedford Castle in 1224.) At Orford the bailey has vanished above ground, the last fragment of wall (page 19) collapsing 'with a tremendous crash' at ten minutes after eleven o'clock on the night of Thursday 1 July 1841. (Information supplied by courtesy of Major Steuart Gratton from a contemporary note by Dr Samuel Randall.) The fortunate survival of John Norden's survey of 1600–02, however, enables us to obtain some impression of the castle when it still remained more or less complete (page 8). The most interesting feature of Norden's view, which is drawn from the south-west, is the series of rectangular mural towers shown projecting at intervals from the outer curtain wall. Since there is no evidence of their building at any later time in the history of Orford, and since their rectangular form suggests a twelfth-century date, it may be presumed that they formed part of the original work of 1165–73. If so, the point is worth noting, for the exploitation of the mural or flanking tower, a Classical technique, was one of the most important developments in medieval military architecture. It solved the problem of defending a long stretch of wall without exposing the defenders themselves, for it broke the wall up into sections, each overtopped and commanded by a pair of towers which, projecting forward into the field, also enabled cross-fire to be directed upon the wall's exposed outer face and base. Used and placed systematically, in fact, the mural or flanking tower enabled the bailey, or the whole enclosure of the castle, to be adequately defended. Thus the castle could become, in terms of defence, one integrated unit, as is most perfectly seen in the great Edwardian castles of over a century later, Caernarfon, Conwy, Caerphilly or the fully developed Tower of London. Mural towers were used in the timber defences of some early castles, and eleventh-century stone-built examples occur at Ludlow in Shropshire, or at Richmond in Yorkshire, but one of the earliest surviving examples of their extensive and systematic use in England

The castle, the town and Orford Ness in the time of Elizabeth I

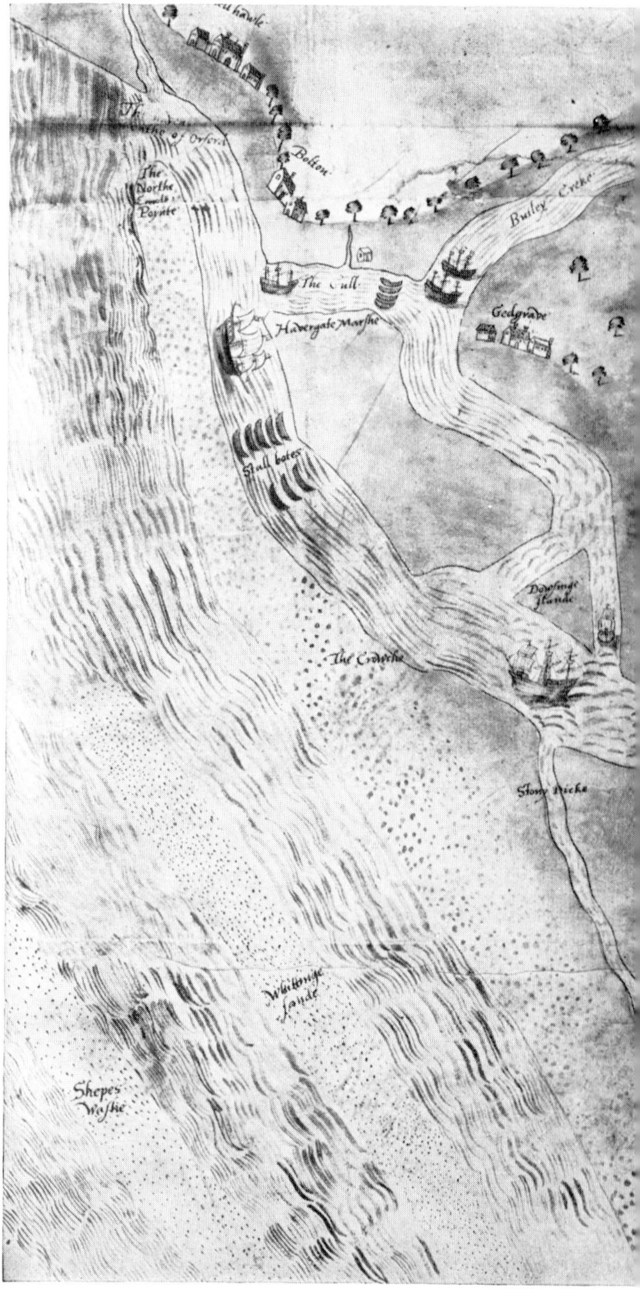

Chapmans
The Lazer howse
Orforde
Sudbourne
The Londes Marshe

is in the inner and outer curtain walls at Dover, built by Henry II between *c*1168 and *c*1180. They are also found, impressively and systematically employed, at Framlingham in Suffolk, rebuilt by Earl Roger Bigod in *c*1190. At both Dover and Framlingham the towers are rectangular and otherwise closely resemble one another, but it would seem more likely that the Bigod towers are based upon those at nearby Orford. (There are other affinities between Framlingham and Orford, notably the triangular joggled arches found both in the main gateway of the former and in the entrance to the keep of the latter (page 17).)

The keep at Orford may also be thought of as advanced, or at any rate very interesting in its design. It is cylindrical inside but polygonal outside, the whole buttressed and strengthened by three rectangular projecting turrets (the south adjoining a forebuilding) rising to battlemented tops above the battlemented summit of the main tower (page 7). By contrast, the characteristic twelfth-century keep in England was a great rectangular tower, such as may be seen in East Anglia at Norwich and Castle Rising in Norfolk, at Castle Hedingham and Colchester (the latter late eleventh-century) in Essex, or the ruined Bigod keep at Bungay in Suffolk. Henry II himself was a notable builder of such donjons, at Scarborough in Yorkshire (*c*1159–68), for example, or at Bridgnorth in Shropshire (*c*1166–74), at the Peak in Derbyshire (*c*1170), at Newcastle upon Tyne (*c*1172–77), and at Dover, Kent (*c*1180–90), his greatest and his finest. Orford keep (1165–67), though in fact ante-dating some of these, is often labelled 'transitional,' standing in the supposed sequence of English donjons, as it were, mid-way between the rectangular towers and the cylindrical towers usually associated with the thirteenth century, such as Pembroke, Longtown, Skenfrith, Bronllys, Tretower or Flint, all in Wales and the Marches, or Launceston in Cornwall. However, New Buckenham in Norfolk can show the remains of a cylindrical keep of about 1150 and therefore earlier than most of the rectangular great towers in the country, and there are others as early or earlier in France, some of them attributed to Henry II himself. Orford, it may be suggested, is not meaningfully 'transitional' but simply neither square nor round, and is best compared with others not entirely dissimilar nor entirely uncommon in its period—with Henry's keeps, for example, at Chilham in Kent, Tickhill in Yorkshire, and Gisors in Normandy, or with Earl Hamelin de Warenne's Conisbrough (Yorks),

Comparative plans of twelfth-century keeps

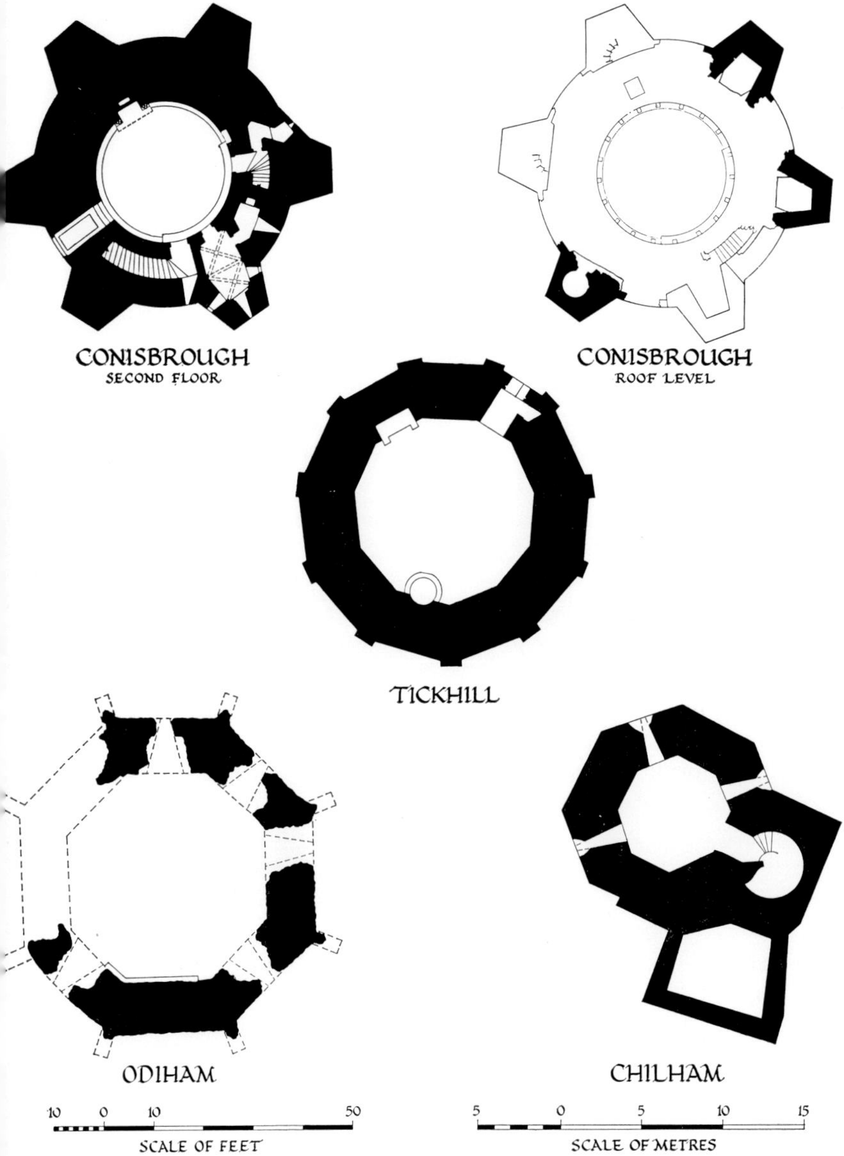

or King John's Odiham in Hampshire (see page 15). Even so, it yet differs from them all in the details of its overall design, and is, in short, unique.

The keep at Orford stands upon a great battered plinth (i.e. a splayed-out thickening at the base), and rises to a height of some 90ft (27m) from ground level to the original summit of its battlemented turrets, the walls of the central tower itself being some 10ft (3m) thick. The whole is built principally of local septaria (a soft, Clayey limestone), now much worn but originally cut and laid in large square blocks. Freestone ashlar (chiefly oolite externally and Caen stone internally) was, however, used for the plinth and for the battlements, for the string-courses and the dressings of all openings, and for the quoins which mark each external angle of the tower. The lower part of the south side of the keep is also faced in freestone ashlar above the plinth. Internally the keep is divided into a basement and two principal storeys, each storey comprising a hall or main apartment occupying the entire space of the tower proper, with subsidiary rooms and chambers in the northern and western turrets. The third or southern turret contains the splendid newel or spiral staircase, which rises sheer from the basement to the summit and gives access to the rooms at every level. Adjoining this southern turret is the forebuilding, with the entrance to the keep at first-floor level, and with its own basement below this, and the chapel above. The forebuilding rises to little above half the height of the main tower; its roof is battlemented, and no doubt provided a useful fighting platform. The original roof of the tower proper was conical (see cross-section at end of guide), springing from corbels which can still be seen in the hall of the second storey, and probably rising little if at all above the level of the wall and turrets of the keep, which thus protected it from the projectiles of besieging forces. Seen from the outside, the principal windows of the two main storeys above the basement are all of two orders, the outer being round-headed and with a solid tympanum, the inner square-headed (except in the vestibule of the forebuilding where they are again round) with a heavy quadrant moulding. The three basement windows were probably at first mere narrow loops like all the other minor windows of the keep, but they have evidently been cut back at some later date to a width which absorbs most of the ashlar quoins through which they emerge. Just above ground level, on the west side of the keep in the angle between the tower and the west turret, there is a fine battery of four round-headed shoots for the ejection of the spoil from the four garderobes incorporated in the upper levels of the same turret.

One enters the keep, now as always, through a doorway with a curious triangular joggled arch, at first-floor level on the south-west side of the forebuilding. The external steps leading up to this doorway are modern (Napoleonic?), but perhaps do not differ greatly from the former arrangements, except that there may originally have been a break and drawbridge. Immediately within the doorway, the grooves for the portcullis can be seen, leading up to the chapel above. Thus entered, one finds oneself in a kind of entrance vestibule, originally well lighted. Beneath is a basement, reached only by a wooden ladder, and having no connection with the main basement of the main tower and no other means of access. In its south wall are the remains of a ventilating shaft sloping steeply upwards through the thickness of the wall, to emerge externally above the plinth, where its opening was originally covered by a metal grille with closely spaced bars. From the north end of this basement an angled passage leads to what was once a garderobe recess. The lower part of this recess, including the seat, has later been broken through to give access, behind and at a lower level, to a low barrel-vaulted chamber, which was once the cess-pit for the garderobe. While it is generally advisable to take with a pinch of salt those guides and guidebooks avidly describing medieval castles in terms of prisoners languishing in dark and dismal 'dungeons,' the isolation of this basement room, its garderobe and its barred ventilation shaft, all point to the possibility of its occasional use for the incarceration of recalcitrant prisoners.

From the entrance vestibule, beneath a splendid triple arch fanning out from left to right, steps which pass beneath two more triangular joggled arches—and which formerly passed through two pairs of double doors—lead into the great hall or principal apartment of the first-floor residential suite. The hall itself is large, circular and impressive, occupying the entire inner circumference of the tower. A stone bench runs round its walls, and to the right of the doorway on entering there are two round-headed wall-recesses with further benches. There is a fireplace, altered in the later Middle Ages but perhaps originally surmounted by a tall stone hood, and the room is very well lighted by three great window openings, each with double round-headed lights set back in deep recesses whose own arches are slightly pointed. Each of these recesses gives access to the various subsidiary chambers and offices which served this hall, and which in fact are ingeniously constructed within the north and west turrets of the tower. Thus the south-west window recess, to the left of the entrance, contains a short passage leading into a kitchen, which has a double fireplace or oven, and a sink and drain at waist level. Another passage on the far side of the kitchen now leads to a double garderobe with a partition wall between the seats, though this access to the garderobes from the kitchen results from a later alteration; they were entered originally from the hall. The window recess on the opposite, eastern side of the wall has a passage, with a small window opening, leading into a chamber which is lit by a single window, and is in fact situated in the northern turret behind the fireplace of the hall. The third window recess to the left of the fireplace gives access to a newel staircase leading up to another chamber in the north turret directly above the one just described. This upper chamber has often been assigned to the constable, the resident commandant of the castle. The passage at the head of the stairs leading into it has a small window aperture and the interesting feature of a urinal neatly worked in stone through the thickness of the wall (*cf* the urinal at Castle Rising, Norfolk). The chamber itself has a single window light.

Descending from the 'constable's chamber,' visitors will find, diametrically opposite on the south side of the hall, the doorway leading out to the main newel staircase of the keep. Constructed in the southern turret, this spacious staircase, 5ft 6in (1.7m) wide, has suffered very little damage except at the top and otherwise still appears much as it was built some 800 years ago. Downwards it leads to the main basement of the keep, again circular in plan, with two deep recesses opening out of it into the basements of the northern and western turrets, and lit by three deeply splayed and shelving window openings. Used chiefly for storage, it has no architectural features of particular interest except the well at its centre, and, to the right of the entrance, a stone sink with a drain or aqueduct running off from it through the thickness of the wall. The well itself, an essential feature of a keep designed for self-sufficient residence and defence, is a superb piece of medieval engineering, smoothly cased in stone and some 32ft (9.7m) deep.

Reascending the spiral staircase, visitors will next reach, at a level half-way between the first and second main storeys of the keep, a passageway leading off on the left to the chapel and the chaplain's chamber. The chapel forms the upper level of the forebuilding, directly above the entrance vestibule beneath it. It is, and was meant to

The castle from the south-east, from an engraving of 1785 by S Hooper

be, a beautiful little place, well lit and with arcaded walls, and these features, together with its (ruined) altar, its piscina and its aumbries, seem to give access to the living past more directly perhaps than any other spot in Orford. The passage which leads to the chapel leads past it to the chaplain's chamber, lit by a single window, and on the far side of this is his private garderobe, among the best preserved of all the sanitary arrangements in the keep.

A little further up the main staircase, a broader passage, again on one's left, leads past a doorway (now a window) giving access to the chapel roof, and into the apartments of the second storey of the keep. This residential suite was probably the grander of the two, intended for the more important visitors to the castle, including the King himself. It consists, like the first-storey suite below it, of a great circular hall with subsidiary chambers and offices opening off its three deep, two-lighted window recesses. The fireplace, like the one below it, has been altered in the later Middle Ages from its original form, and now has a moulded segmental head, flanked by half-octagonal attached shafts supported by crudely carved heads and carrying moulded capitals. A short passage from the window recess to the left of the entrance leads, as on the floor below, to a kitchen constructed in the west turret, this time with a single fireplace or oven and a drain at floor level. On this floor there is a single garderobe reached by a passage from the window recess to the left of the fireplace, and opposite, on the other side of the same recess, another passage leads into a chamber in the north turret, provided with a single window and a floor-level drain. The remaining window recess has on either side a deep closet or cupboard, each lit by a small window opening, and intended perhaps for the deposit and safekeeping of valuables. Round the circumference of the great hall, at a height of some 8ft (2.4m) from the floor, a ring of strong corbels jut out from the wall, each surmounted by a chase cut in ashlar to take a steeply raking joist. Though it has formerly been suggested that these once supported a timber gallery, there is in fact no doubt that from them originally sprang the supports of a conical roof, whose rain-water drain or conduit can still be seen piercing the thickness of the wall opposite the fireplace at a point above the level of the corbels. It follows that the isolated chamber in the north turret, whose entrance can now be seen well above and to the left of the fireplace, was originally outside the roof and must have been entered from a catwalk about its base. There is another similarly isolated chamber at the same level in the west turret, reached by a long narrow passage, traversed by the conduit from the original roof, and leading off from the main staircase at a point just below the battlements. Though often identified as dovecotes (which indeed most castles contained) because of certain holes punched through the walls and visible in the west turret, it is clear that neither chamber was originally constructed as such. They may have provided shelter for men and supplies needed on the battlements, though there is also a possibility that the chamber in the western turret at the end of the passage, which alone among the chambers in the keep is stepped down and cased half-way up its walls with dressed stone (and whose entrance has also at some point been altered), may have been a cistern such as is found at the summit of the near-contemporary keep at Conisbrough.

Finally the main newel staircase ascends to the modern flat roof of the great tower. Above this level the three turrets rise again to their own battlemented tops. On the west turret some of the battlements are sufficiently well preserved for the grooves, which once took the wooden shutters swinging between the merlons, to be seen. (There is another well-preserved example of this feature on the chapel roof.) In their last storey the three turrets provide further shelter and storage space for the defenders on the battlements, and in the north turret there is an oven, such as is found again at the top of the keep at Conisbrough. But the chief reward, perhaps, for visitors who have climbed so high, is the wide, wind-swept view of Orford and Orford Ness, the sea and the marsh-lands of the Suffolk coast, over which Henry II's keep has stood sentinel now for eight long centuries.

The earthwork defences of the castle now extend south-westwards from the keep for a distance of some 180yd (165m), but it is possible that more existed to the east where they may have been destroyed by the encroachment of the town. The keep itself stands on a platform circled by a ditch beyond which is a rampart. This probably formed a complete circle round the keep, although the north-eastern side towards the town is now missing. Outside the rampart are a second ditch and a second and slighter rampart, well preserved only on the north-west, west and south-west. A third ditch separates this rampart from a small earthwork platform still further to the south-west, and beyond this again there was perhaps a small spur work, but the ground here has been much disturbed by quarrying and the evidence is uncertain.

The Orford Merman

No guide to Orford Castle is complete without the tale of the Orford Merman caught by local fishermen in the time of Bartholomew de Glanville, the first constable (appointed 1167, see page 5). It was first told by the chronicler Ralph of Coggeshall (*fl* 1207) in his *Chronicon Anglicanum:*

'In the time of King Henry II, when Bartholomew de Glanville was custodian of the Castle, it happened that the fishermen, fishing in the sea, caught in their nets a wild man, whom in their wonder they brought to the Castellan. He was naked and was like a man in all his members. He was covered with hair and had a long and shaggy beard. The knight kept him in custody many days and nights, lest he should return to the sea. He eagerly ate whatever was brought to him, whether raw or cooked, but the raw he pressed between his hands until all the juice was expelled. Whether he would or could not, he would not talk, although oft-times hung up by his feet and harshly tortured. Brought into the church, he showed no signs of reverence or belief either by genuflexion or bending of the head when he saw the sacred elements. He sought his bed at sunset and always remained there until sunrise.

'It happened that once they brought him to the harbour and suffered him to go into the sea, strongly guarding him with three lines of nets; but he dived under the nets out into the deep sea, and came up again and again as if in derision of the spectators on the shore. After thus playing about for a long while, when they had almost given up hope of his return, he came back of his own free will. But later on, being negligently guarded, he secretly fled to the sea and was never afterwards seen.'

Glossary

ASHLAR	Squared block(s) of stone.
AUMBRY	A cupboard or recess in a wall, in which to place sacramental vessels.
BAILEY	A courtyard or ward of a castle.
BATTER	The inclined face of a wall.
CAPITAL	Decorated member between an arch and the pillar or support from which it springs.
CORBEL	Stone bracket projecting from a wall, intended to support a weight.
CURTAIN	A wall enclosing a courtyard.
DONJON	Great tower or keep.
FOREBUILDING	A projection containing the stairs leading to the first floor of a keep.
JOGGLED	Irregular jointing to provide a key.
KEEP	Great tower or donjon.
MERLON	The solid part of an embattled parapet between openings; sometimes pierced with slits.
MOTTE	A castle mound of earth or turf.
MURAL TOWER	Tower constructed on the curtain wall and projecting out from it.
NEWEL STAIRS	Spiral stairs.
PISCINA	A basin with a drain in a wall-niche, used for cleansing sacramental vessels.
PLINTH	Projecting masonry at the base of a wall.
PORTCULLIS	An iron-shod wooden grille suspended by chains in grooves in front of a gate, and let down in time of necessity.
QUOINS	Squared stones used to finish the corner of a building.
RAMPART	Mass of excavated earth on which the troops and guns of the garrison were elevated.
STRING-COURSE	Horizontal band of masonry, usually projecting from the wall.
TYMPANUM	Space between the lintel of a doorway and an arch above it.

Printed in Scotland by Her Majesty's Stationery Office at HMSO Press, Edinburgh
Dd 586061 K96 5/78 (15149)